Wired

ANASTASIA SUEN

Illustrated by

PAUL CARRICK

Charlesbridge

humming, thrumming,

Electricity starts with something you cannot see: electrons. Electrons are part of an atom, and atoms are inside everything, including you!

Electricity is electrons on the move. To create electricity we make electrons move on purpose. The electricity that you use every day moves on wires that run all over the city.

But one electron does not travel from a power plant straight to your house. Oh, no! When electrons move, they dance in circles. As the electrons dance, electricity flows from one electron to another. The electrons dance the electricity from the power plant all the way to your house. As long as the electrons keep dancing, electricity can keep flowing.

power's coming

At the power plant, machines make power by making electrons move. As water flows through the dam, it makes big wheels, called turbines, spin. The turbines are connected to a generator. Inside the generator is a large magnet surrounded with wires. When the turbines spin, the magnet spins, too. As the magnet spins, the electrons in the wires begin to move. Electricity has been created!

dam

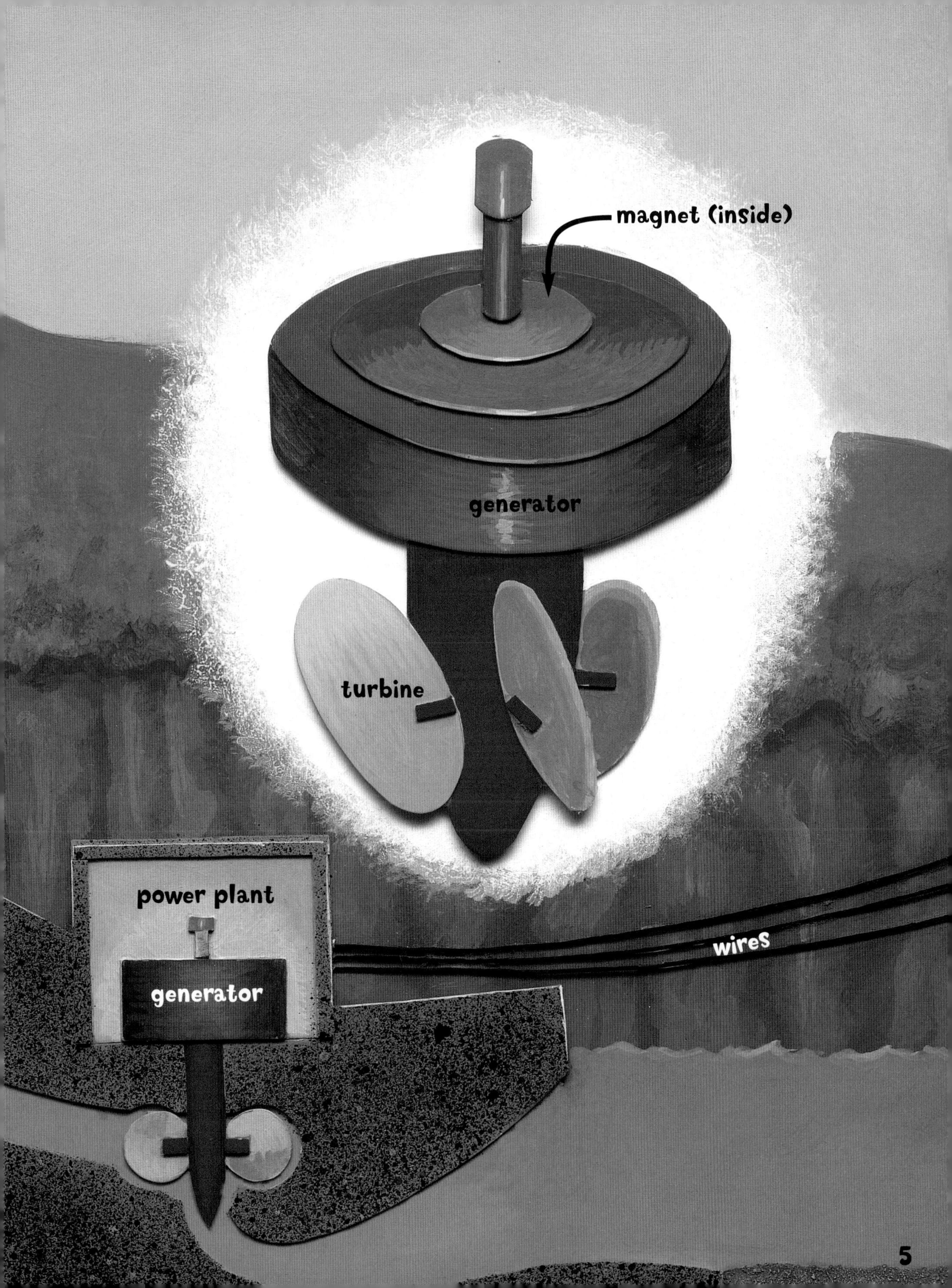

magnet (inside)

generator

turbine

power plant

generator

wires

Outside the power plant, the wires from the generator connect to a step-up transformer. Inside the transformer, two coils of wire circle around a core. One coil is longer than the other, so it goes around the core more times. The electricity enters the transformer on the smaller coil. This creates a magnetic field, so the electrons on the longer coil start dancing, too! Since the longer coil circles the core more times, the electricity is "stepped up."

Stepped-up electricity has more voltage. Voltage is like pressure in a hose: the more water you have flowing through the hose at once, the stronger the spray and the higher the pressure. The more electrons you have moving through a wire, the higher the voltage. The three wires coming out of the step-up transformer are called high-voltage lines.

in the wires

The high-voltage lines from the step-up transformer are carried on tall towers called transmission towers. Transmit means "to send."

The electrons in these wires dance the electricity from one place to the next. Transmission towers carry high-voltage wires for miles and miles. The voltage these lines carry is very high. When electricity comes into the step-up transformer, it is 13,000 to 24,000 volts. After the electricity is stepped up, it can be as high as 345,000 volts!

transmission
towers

from big to small to power it all

When the high-voltage wires come near a city, some branch off to a branch station, or substation. At the substation, the wires come down to earth and connect to another transformer. This transformer will "step down" the voltage.

A step-down transformer also has two coils of wires around a core. The wires coming in from the high-voltage lines connect to the longer coil. As the electrons on the longer coil dance, they create a magnetic field inside the transformer. This makes the electrons in the smaller coil start dancing, too. The smaller coil has fewer turns around the core, so the voltage (the pressure) has been stepped down.

Now it's time to feed the hungry city! Distribution lines, or "feeder" lines, reach out all across the city. These lines distribute power to everyone in the city who needs it.

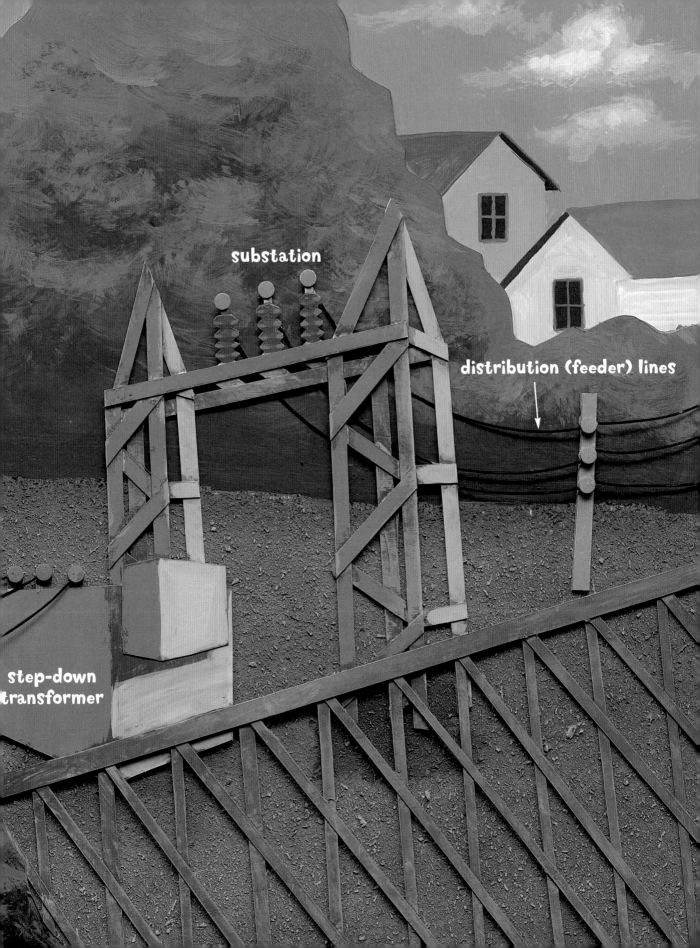

substation

distribution (feeder) lines

step-down transformer

with the wires
with the wires

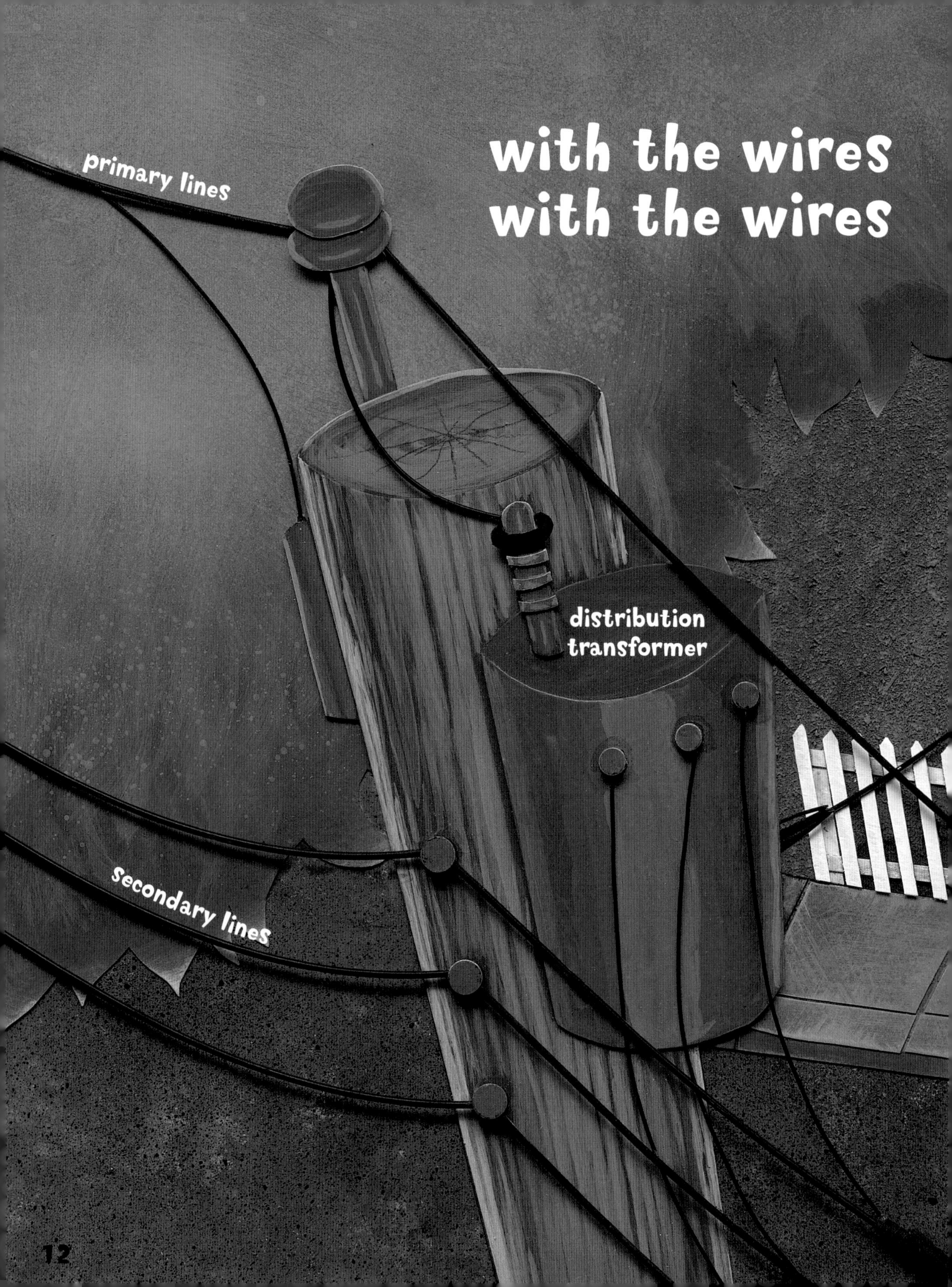

primary lines

distribution
transformer

secondary lines

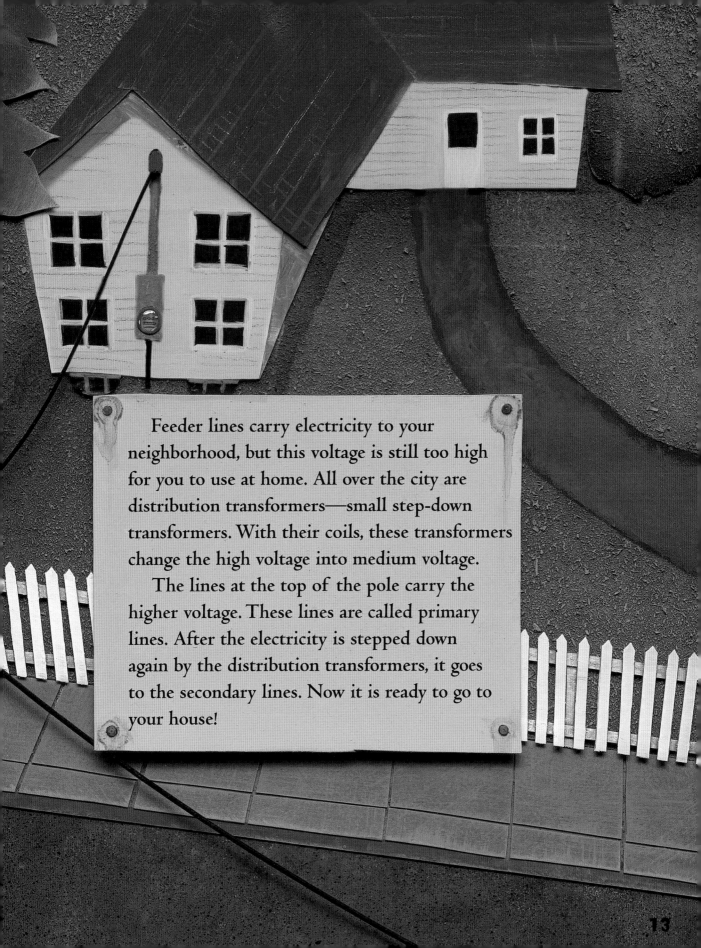

Feeder lines carry electricity to your neighborhood, but this voltage is still too high for you to use at home. All over the city are distribution transformers—small step-down transformers. With their coils, these transformers change the high voltage into medium voltage.

The lines at the top of the pole carry the higher voltage. These lines are called primary lines. After the electricity is stepped down again by the distribution transformers, it goes to the secondary lines. Now it is ready to go to your house!

one for each
the wires reach

The secondary lines reach each building in the city at a service head. Wires from the power company connect to wires from your house. These wires don't carry 345,000 or 24,000 or 13,000 volts anymore. They only carry 120 volts—just right for your house. (That's still dangerous voltage, so don't touch!)

The wires travel down through a conduit to the electric meter. The electric meter measures how much electricity travels to each building.

Below the meter is a grounding rod. (Every power pole has one, too!) Believe it or not, the dirt in the ground is a safety feature. Too much electricity flowing in the wires can cause a fire. To prevent this, a copper wire is attached to a rod in the ground. If too much power flows in the wires, the "grounding" wire carries the extra power to the rod and into the ground.

service head

conduit

electric meter

grounding rod

see the wires
see the wires

Three wires travel through the electric meter to the service entrance. Two wires are "hot" wires and one is "neutral." After you use the electricity, the electrons keep dancing—only now they dance out of your house on the neutral wire. The path electricity makes as it travels from beginning to end and then back again is called a circuit.

grounding ro

Service
entrance

into the wall to power it all

The next stop for the dancing electrons is inside your house. The two hot wires, the neutral wire, and the grounding wire go through the wall to the service panel. Here the wires reach the main breaker.

A breaker is a switch that can stop the power. If something goes wrong with the electricity, the breaker pops and breaks the circuit. It makes a gap so the wires no longer touch. When that happens, the power stops flowing. The main breaker can turn all the power for your house on or off.

The electrician who put the wires inside the walls of your house didn't make one long path or circuit for the whole house. Oh, no! He created many, many paths. Each one has a breaker in the service panel. The labels on the panel door tell you where the circuits travel.

Service panel

OFF

main breaker

ON

breaker

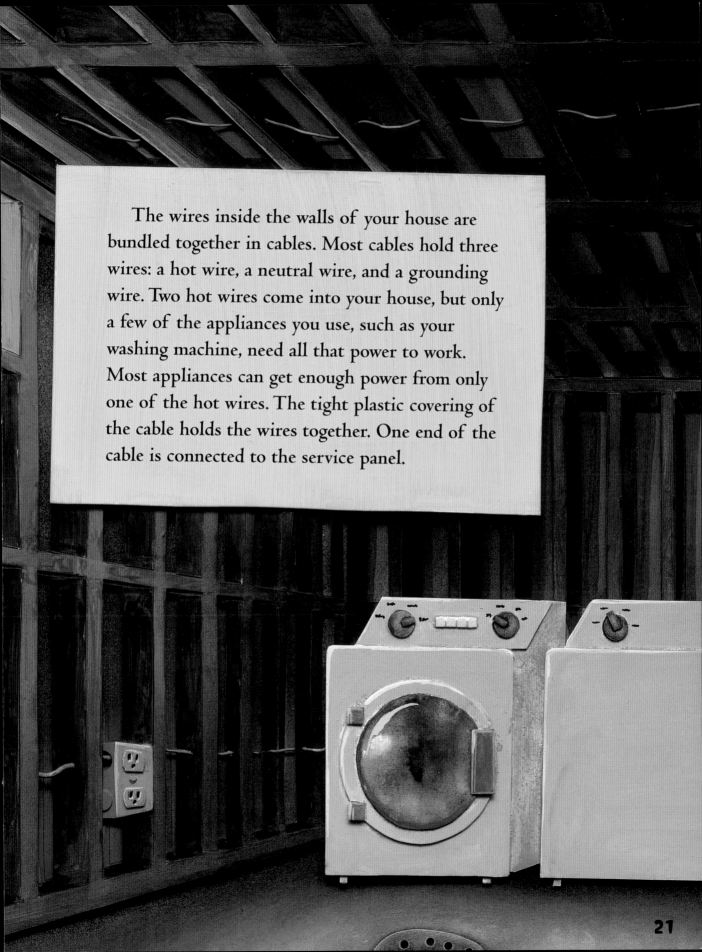

The wires inside the walls of your house are bundled together in cables. Most cables hold three wires: a hot wire, a neutral wire, and a grounding wire. Two hot wires come into your house, but only a few of the appliances you use, such as your washing machine, need all that power to work. Most appliances can get enough power from only one of the hot wires. The tight plastic covering of the cable holds the wires together. One end of the cable is connected to the service panel.

box

neutral

hot wire

wire nut

ground

neutral

hot

ground

ground

switch

hot

click! on it goes the power flows

Each cable travels through the wall until it reaches a box. Inside the hollow box, the three wires from the cable are connected to switches or outlets. Switches connect power from the service panel to an appliance, like a light on your ceiling.

To make a switch work, the electrician connects a hot wire from the cables on each side of the box to the two screws on the far side of the switch. The neutral wires are twisted together in a wire nut. The wire nut keeps the wires touching, so the electricity can keep flowing back through the circuit. The grounding wires from the two cables are also connected by a wire nut. A third grounding wire extends from the wire nut to a screw on the near side of the switch. This grounds the switch.

When you flip the switch on, it closes the gap between the wires inside the switch. The electricity moves from one wire to the next and the power flows! When you flip the switch off, it makes a gap so the wires are no longer touching and the electricity stops.

lamps glow
heaters blow

outlet

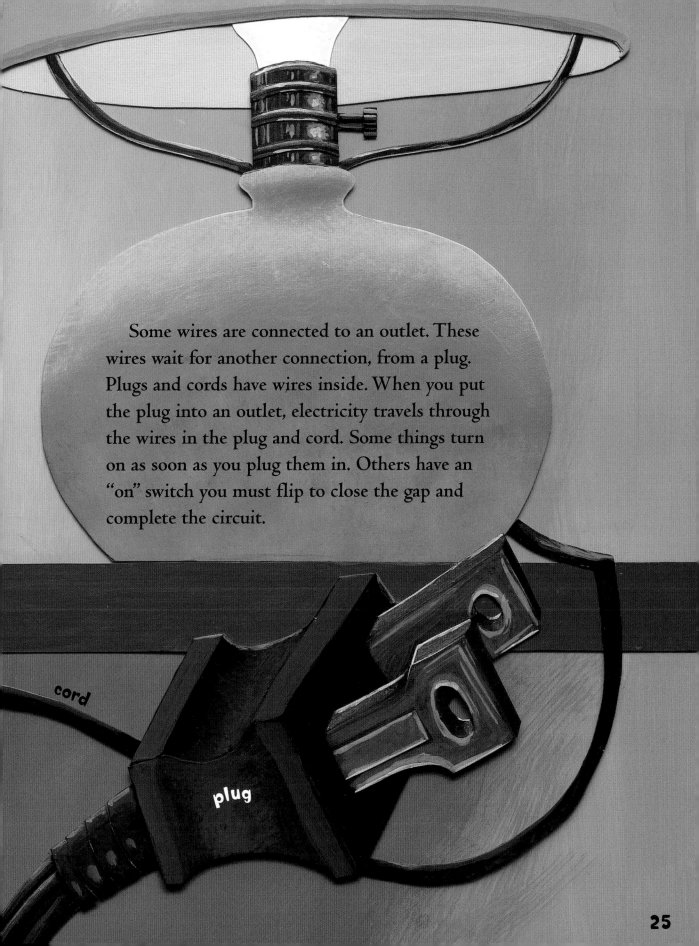

Some wires are connected to an outlet. These wires wait for another connection, from a plug. Plugs and cords have wires inside. When you put the plug into an outlet, electricity travels through the wires in the plug and cord. Some things turn on as soon as you plug them in. Others have an "on" switch you must flip to close the gap and complete the circuit.

cord

plug

clocks tick
computers click

WIRED!

Electricity is always on the move.
As electrons dance in circles, they move
electricity from the power plant to your
house and back. As long as the electrons
keep dancing through the wires,
electricity keeps flowing!

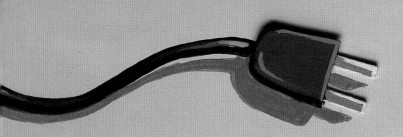

Be smart about power!

- Don't get close to power lines.

- Don't dig near underground power lines.

- Don't play near electric power boxes.

- Don't fly a kite near power lines.

- Don't play with outlets.

- Don't plug too many things into an outlet.

- To unplug a machine, pull from the

  plug only. Don't pull the cord.

- Don't use cords that are torn or frayed.

- Don't put a cord in water.

- Don't put cords under rugs.

Find out more!

Electrical Safety Foundation International (ESFi)
http://www.esfi.org/index.php

How Power Grids Work
http://science.howstuffworks.com/power.htm

Bang, Molly. *My Light*. New York: Blue Sky Press, 2004.
   The sun explains light and energy.

Cole, Joanna. *The Magic School Bus and the Electric Field Trip*.
   New York: Scholastic Press, 1997. Ms. Frizzle takes a
   field trip through the town's electrical wires.

Seuling, Barbara. *Flick a Switch: How Electricity Gets to Your
   Home*. New York: Holiday House, 2003. The discovery
   and use of electricity.

Glossary / Index

atom: the smallest unit of matter. Atoms contain electrons. *p. 3*

box: a container in a wall where wires connect to switches or outlets. *pp. 22, 23*

branch station: *See* substation.

breaker, circuit breaker: a switch that allows or stops the flow of electric current. *p. 18*

cable: a group of wires bound together. *pp. 20, 21, 23*

circuit: a path that electricity follows from beginning to end and back again. *pp. 16, 18, 23, 25*

conduit: a pipe that holds wires. *p. 14*

cord: a flexible electric wire with a plug attached. *p. 25*

distribution ("feeder") lines: wires that carry electricity from the substation to cities and towns. *pp. 10, 11, 13*

distribution transformer: a machine that lowers the voltage so people can use electricity safely. *pp. 12, 13*

electric meter: a machine that measures the amount of electric power used. *pp. 14, 15, 16*

electricity: energy made available by the flow of electrons. *pp. 3, 4, 6, 8, 14, 16, 23, 25*

electrons: the part of an atom that moves an electric current. *pp. 3, 4, 6, 8, 10, 14, 16, 18, 26*

generator: a machine that makes electric power. *pp. 4, 5, 6*

grounding rod: a rod outside your house that carries extra electric current into the earth. *pp. 14, 15, 17*

grounding wire: the wire in every plug that carries extra electric current out of the house to the grounding rod. *pp. 14, 18, 21, 22, 23*

high-voltage lines: wires that carry electricity from the power plant to substations in the city. *pp. 6, 7, 8, 10*

hot wire: one of a pair of wires that allows electric current into your house. *pp. 16, 18, 21, 22, 23*

magnet: a metal object that attracts other objects. *pp. 4, 5*

magnetic field: an area of energy that develops around a magnet. *pp. 6, 10*

neutral wire: the third wire that keeps the electrons moving in a complete circuit. *pp. 16, 18, 21, 22, 23*

outlet: a receptacle in a wall that is connected to a power supply and that has a socket for a plug. *pp. 23, 24, 25*

plug: a fitting with metal prongs that fits in an outlet and connects an appliance to a power supply. *p. 25*

power plant: a large station that generates electricity for a city or region. *pp. 3, 4, 5, 6*

primary lines: the power lines that carry electricity to the distribution transformer. *pp. 12, 13*

secondary lines: the power lines that carry electricity out of the distribution transformer. *pp. 12, 13, 14*

service entrance: where the wires from the electric meter enter your house. *pp. 16, 17*

service head: where the wires from the power company reach your house to provide power. *p. 14*

service panel: the box on the wall where the wires from the electric meter connect to circuits in your house. *pp. 18, 19, 21, 23*

step-down transformer: a machine that lowers the voltage of the electricity. *pp. 10, 11, 13*

step-up transformer: a machine that raises the voltage of the electricity. *pp. 6, 7, 8*

substation: a station where the power from the transmission line is lowered for use in the city. *pp. 10, 11*

switch: a device used to connect or block the flow of the electric current. *pp. 22, 23, 25*

transformer: a machine that raises or lowers the voltage of electric current. *pp. 6, 13*

transmission towers: tall towers that hold up high-voltage lines. *pp. 8, 9*

transmit: to send by wire. *p. 8*

turbine: a machine that spins when water passes over it. *pp. 4, 5*

voltage: the amount of strength or pressure in electric current. *pp. 6, 10, 13*

wire nut: a small cover for wires that keeps the ends touching. *pp. 22, 23*

wire: a metallic strand or rod used to carry an electric charge. *pp. 4, 6, 8, 10, 14, 16, 18, 21, 23, 25*

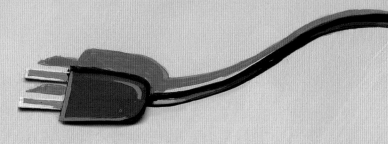

For my science teachers, Mr. Frank and Brother Vincent, and for science teachers everywhere!

With special thanks to Joe E. Hackney, C. E. T.
—A. S.

For Dr. Duggles, the self-zappa
—P. C.

Text copyright © 2007 by Anastasia Suen
Illustrations copyright © 2007 by Paul Carrick

Published by Charlesbridge
85 Main Street
Watertown, MA 02472
(617) 926-0329
www.charlesbridge.com

Library of Congress Cataloging-in-Publication Data
Suen, Anastasia.
    Wired / Anastasia Suen ; illustrated by Paul Carrick.
        p. cm.
    Summary: "Describes how electricity is conducted and follows its route
from a power plant to the home. Includes glossary."—Provided by publisher.
    ISBN: 978-1-57091-599-4 (reinforced for library use)
    ISBN: 978-1-57091-494-2 (softcover)
1. Electric power—Juvenile literature. 2. Electricity—Juvenile literature.
I. Carrick, Paul. II. Title.
TK148.S827 2006
621.319—dc22   2005019623

Printed in China

(hc) 10 9 8 7 6 5 4 3 2 1
(sc) 10 9 8 7 6 5 4 3 2 1

Illustrations done in acrylic mixed media on white styrene plasticard
Text type set in Monotype Centaur and display type set in Softie by Tail Spin Studio
Color transparencies of 3-D art shot by Gamma One, NYC
Color separations by Chroma Graphics, Singapore
Printed and bound by Jade Productions
Production supervision by Brian G. Walker
Designed by Susan Mallory Sherman